Five Ways of Healing from an Amputation

Book written by Anthony Taylor
Cover and book layout by Terry Tomlinson
Editing by Rebekah Icenesse
This cover has been designed using assets from Freepik.com.

Manufactured in the United States of America

PUBLISHING CONCEPTS LLC

For more information, please contact:
Publishing Concepts LLC
6590 Scanlan Avenue
St. Louis, MO 63139
www.PublishingConceptsLLC.com

PAPERBACK ISBN: 978-1-957307-12-1
EBOOK (PDF) ISBN: 978-1-57307-13-8

SELF-HELP TECHNIQUES

1 2 3 4 5 6 7 8 9 10

Dedication

I want to dedicate this book to people who were
born with limb loss and do not understand why they
were born this way. I want you to know that you
are here for a reason, so do not lose hope. Amazing
people like you give people like me the hope and the
courage to live life after amputation without limitations.

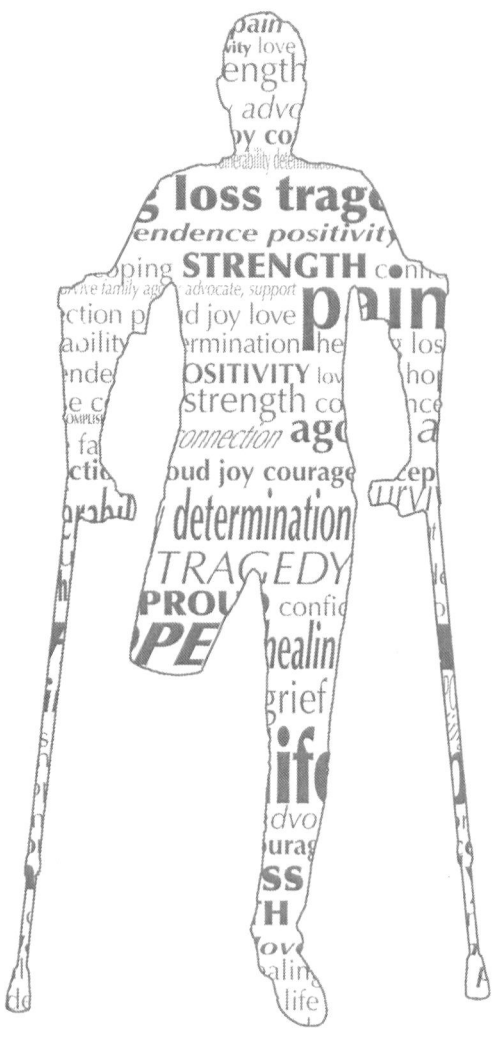

Table of Contents

Acknowledgments

First off, I want to thank God for sparing my life, and I want to give a special thanks to everybody who prayed for me during that difficult time. And to all my supporters, I want to say thanks from the bottom of my heart. You are the reason I go hard every day to make a difference in my community and someone else's life. To my fiancé and friends, thanks for always believing in me, even when I didn't believe in myself. My granny girl, I do not know what I would do without you. You are a brave woman, and I believe I get my strength from you because you show me each day there is nothing I cannot accomplish.

I want to also thank Dr. Catherine Wittgen, who waived all doctor fees for my follow-up appointments, for ensuring that every part of my body was properly healed, and for doing all the evaluations for me to receive my prosthetic.

You know I cannot leave out Premier Prosthetics and my guy, Manny Rivera, who made me feel like family the first day I met him. Manny and his team are the best prosthesis group in the world. They go above and beyond for their patients and show that they care about their patients' journeys and ensure that they are living out their dreams.

And to my one and only mentor, Barbara Nyarady. Every day I ask myself where my life would be without you. Ever since I met you ten years ago when I asked you to be my mentor, you have been in my corner. The work you do is unbelievable, as is the time you spend helping me reach my goals. Your heart went out to me when I told you about my accident. You did not lose faith in me, and we just got the ball rolling again. I thank you so much for continuing to believe in me.

To my Shack family, words cannot describe how much your generosity meant to me and my family as we endured this hardship, and the work that y'all do to always give back is not unnoticed. I love you guys from the bottom of my heart, and your support means the world to me. Brant Baldanza, you are such an incredible person. I cannot thank you enough for answering my texts and the many phone calls we had. It was your jokes that got me through those days. I thought I was not going to make it. Man, I appreciate you.

And to my Cooper's Hawk family for the last nine years, it will take a million books to put into words all I need to say. Y'all always know how to show up and show it through our relationship that I will always keep y'all dear to my heart. Lindsey Lotts, you have such a big heart when it comes to helping people, and you do so much for so many people. I just appreciate you always keeping me in your thoughts and prayers.

To the University of Missouri St. Louis, one of the most amazing schools that care about its community and has the passion to make a difference in people's lives. Thanks for your prayers and the many phone calls and all the generosity you gave to my family and me. Rodney and Deborah, y'all have been heroes of ours for many years. There is not one person in this family y'all does not believe in, and y'all are willing to provide support in any way possible.

To my kids, it is because of y'all I am making it through this experience each day, even though there are days I just want to stare at walls and break down and cry. It is the hope y'all give to me that makes me realize there is more to accomplish each day. And to my family and friends who probably are mad at me because I did not mention your name, I want you to know you are appreciated more than you can know. There are a lot of wonderful things I could say about my friends and family if I could only put them into words but know y'all are in my heart. My rock, my granny, Ereslene McCullough, you deserve all the good things life can give to you. You know how to carry a family burden without showing that it is weighing you down; your strength amazes me every day.

To St. Louis Public Library for your aims, goals, and beliefs that the library must be a safe place to reach your dreams with the help of your wonderful staff. To Maryann Brickey, thanks for answering my emails and listening to my passion for doing Loss of Limb of Awareness Month with the St. Louis Public Library. You have been a tremendous boost to my spirit, and you make me realize there are people who genuinely care about an amputee's journey. To the O'Bryans, all I can say is thank you. There is not a word to say about how blessed I am to know this family here.

Preface

Last year, I dealt with depression, pain, agony, and also the tragedy of being shot multiple times and losing a limb. Going through all this emotional trauma has been my driving force to write this book. I hope this will help someone else heal after suffering a loss.

Chapter 1

Support: Be an Advocate for Yourself

After you suffer a loss of any kind, you lose a part of yourself, and it could take a lifetime to get it back. In order to start healing from a loss, you must accept yourself as your first support because when others do not come through for you, you must still have your own back. For an amputation, one is not given a funeral or repass for a loss. You are just simply left with feelings balled up inside of you as you suffer the pain that surgery brings. Also, you suffer a lack of family support because people cannot imagine you without a limb.

After getting my left leg amputated and after many surgeries, I woke up to a nurse practitioner telling me about phantom pain. I had no idea what she was saying, but this was when I realized my leg was gone. It was the worst feeling ever, and all I could say was, "This has got to be bullshit!" I began to snap at every hospital staff member that came into my room. That moment changed my life forever. It was then that I knew I had to make a difference for myself by supporting my emotions and my kids, and finishing living out my dreams and goals. That moment brought me to the realization that you have to lose something to gain something.

Even though it seemed like everybody was there for me, I still felt alone, just searching for comfort and answers. People who I thought would always be there did not show up because they lost confidence in me. For me, it was my brother. My brother called me and said, "that he is hurting, and he did not know if he could ever see me like this." Since this call, I have not seen nor heard from him, nor does he answer my calls. He periodically may answer my texts just to say he has been busy, or that he may stop by my house but never shows up. Even though this has been devastating for my kids and shattered their lives without shedding a tear, I still have been that rock for my family, even though I am ripped up inside.

For me, I had to use my voice to start healing myself, to start getting the hurt that was on the inside out of me because the people you love dearly will use and abuse you. I had to be an advocate for myself to not let this amputation take control of my life, so I had to let go and find closure. Even though I was seeing all these doctors and surgeons, I still felt empty as my bloodshot eyes stared at the walls from sleepless nights and the nightmares that make a person want to commit suicide because of all the drama they have been through. The way I started to heal myself was by wanting to learn more about what my doctors were doing at the time of my dressing changes. So, I started getting more involved with the process. Seeing the wound heal started to slowly heal me on the inside. It made me tolerate the hurt and pain that I had endured.

You need to identify what support means to you as you face your disappointment because, at times, you just do not know what to do. There were too many times I tried to hide myself underneath the covers to find out who was there by my side, only to find myself staring at the ceiling and still lying in the bed by myself.

When I started to accept, I was my biggest disappointment. It helped me to understand the circumstances that I put myself in. It also helped me to realize the people I had hurt and to understand how selfish I had been. To find closure for support, one must stop holding unreal expectations of people to be there for you after you endure a life-changing event; people only understand it for the moment while you still have to accept it, let go of it, and live it. I had to learn to support myself and overcome my fear of not having support from others.

Chapter 2

Dealing with Depression: Knowing When to Speak up

Isuffered from depression, and it made me lose sight of who I was as a person. After God spared my life from being shot multiple times and getting my left leg amputated, I felt purposeless and worthless as a person and had thoughts of why I was not dead. Since then, I have lifted myself out of those thoughts by freeing my mind so I can live a life with purpose and meaning. When you have negative thoughts, they take control of your life, and you begin to live out these thoughts. They drive you into a suicidal mindset where you live with this anger and rage where you want somebody else to feel your pain and the hurt that has been done to you. The way I cope with my depression is by getting up and doing something.

For me, it was enrolling back in school, going back to work as a server, and building a solid relationship with my kids by simply telling them that I love them. We all face depression at least once in our lives, but what you do when you're not feeling like yourself is what makes the difference. Only you can answer that question of how to eliminate the hopeless feelings. My depression had me trapped inside my own house, not eating for days, not sleeping for weeks, and taking more medicine than I can count. You need to get up and break this cycle of vulnerability that allows you to be down on yourself and not let it take the best out of you.

I am grateful I went through my depression stage because it allowed me to search for the better me and helped me find the real me again. And even then, with all you go through, you have to figure out the steps that make you whole again because people do not remember what you went through; they only remember where you are in the present. The way I am working through my depression after my amputation is crushing the opinions others have of me and by living my life with no limitations, but also knowing I want to walk as bad as I want to breathe. Those goals alone keep me full of hope and joy.

Chapter 3

Learn How to Cope with Phantom Pain

In all my years of living, I never thought a condition existed called Phantom Pain, so when I heard the doctor and nurses talking about it, I thought it was going to be another surgery I needed after being shot multiple times. Nope, that was not the case at all. It was a pain that hit me in my amputated left leg that made my left leg feel like it was still there. I was screaming at the top of my lungs that I could not take this shit with knots in my stomach while I had a wound vac at the end of my residual limb.

I did not think my hundred twenty-six-pound body could take all the pain I went through. Lying in the hospital for two months and facing the reality that I would never walk again, and this damn phantom pain and all the many surgeries that were happening to me each day I was there, they were all just too much for me.

The game changer happened for me when I began to open up my mouth to ask questions about phantom pain and how they treat it. Also, I wanted to learn more about my dressing changes and what a wound vac was. At that point, I realized I was alive for a reason and a purpose. I got involved in the process of learning how to cope with phantom pain even while the doctor heavily dosed me with gabapentin, a nerve medication to reduce pain, and melatonin to knock my ass out to sleep. It was not until I got home from rehab that I learned how to cope with phantom pain.

My two-year-old son came jumping on me while I was lying in bed dealing with phantom pain. He kicked and jumped on my residual limb shouting, "Daddy!" I guess I was more focused on getting him off me so my girl could give me the gabapentin, and somehow the pain was reduced. I tried all the mirror therapies, and I took gabapentin three times a day. I also rubbed lotion and baby oil on my right leg to stop the phantom pain. They helped somewhat, but what helped the most was when I took my mind off of it, the pain seemed to be less and less. It was not until I took the gabapentin to my kitchen sink, rinsed hot water on them, and then washed them down the drain that my phantom pain completely went away.

Now, I've been getting these crazy charley horses in my left leg. I have to jump up out of my sleep and kick my residual limb out and reposition myself. That is what helps them go away. Lately, I also have been drinking Pedialyte, so I have not had a charley horse in a while. I swear, when you are feeling pain, you want everyone in the world to feel it too. On the other hand, when you allow your pain to heal you and turn it into your passion, it allows you to think differently about the same pain, and it can save your life.

Phantom pain, for me, is just like any other emotion I have. It comes and goes. The more I allow it to hurt me, the longer it stays, but the second I do something about it, it leaves. Coping for me is creating new opportunities for myself and setting goals that are realistic. Also, I have stopped letting people or doctors rate my pain level. A lot of the time, I allowed people to define how I was feeling as if I did not have a damn voice.

When you are in pain, you look for everybody outside of yourself to find comfort. But in the meantime, you are constantly getting disappointed each time around. It was not until I was able to find comfort for myself that I was able to help other people find comfort. The fact of the matter is when you are hurting, the people around you are hurting as well… something to always remember. So, the question I ask myself is if I'm hurting on the inside, why am I faking a front on the outside?

For me, I knew I had to stop the pain on the inside to heal

the people who were hurting the most: my kids, my grandmother, my fiancé, and all my siblings. Too many times, we hide our pain behind medication or become addicted to things. We cover up our pain, never once taking the proper steps to deal with it, and I was the same way. When you fail to take the steps of dealing with your pain, it just shows up on a different day at a different time, just like mine did. My pain caused me sleepless nights. It caused me to be angry and bitter, and it caused me to have thoughts of suicide.

When coping with any form of pain, I try to understand the "why" of it. Once I understand the why, I can take the necessary steps to reduce my pain or deal with my pain. I no longer hide my pain. I simply deal with it so I can help someone else heal. When we do not share our stories about the pain we went through, we leave someone else trapped. You have to get that hurt and pain out of your system. This is the reason I wrote this chapter in my book. If you feel any pain, talk about it, let it out, and you will feel much better. Releasing what is causing you pain makes you feel like yourself again. So, let go of your pain to heal.

Chapter 4

Find Meaning for Your Amputation

When something dramatic happens to us like a life-changing event, usually it leaves us stuck in a shell or a box on what to do. Many times, finding meaning could mean, what could I do to put this behind me? But some people think of retaliation because if they lose something, they feel the world should lose something too. In addition to that, some people are bitter and blame everybody else for their amputation. A lot of us forget that an amputation saves lives, which has been a true reality in my situation. I was not a guy who was in the army, navy, or marines but was shot with an AK-74 and lost my left leg, so for me, a bullet can either take a life or destroy a life.

For me, finding meaning was simply being able to appreciate that all the surgeries went well and that I have more life to live. My amputation allows me to find my real friend, which is myself. It helps me to stop lying to myself, and it helps me to open my heart with love. It gives me some real values that I can live by, such as positivity, commitment, and determination. These are what I live out every day to help my amputation have meaning for me.

One of the most important ideas I would like to talk about in this chapter is K-Levels, which can change how you see physical therapy and occupational therapy and what life is about. What you put in is what you are going to get out of it; the same goes for therapy. I would like for every amputee to be a level K-4 regardless of their age and why they had to get an amputation. I do understand the number one reason for an amputation is diabetes or bad health. Yes, there is an exception if one is simply born with a loss of limb or a different limb. As amputees, we are evaluated on which prosthetic will be suitable for our lifestyle. K-1 is simply going to have you walking with a walker, not doing much if you were active before your amputation. K-2 is simply you walking up and down steps with a cane. K-3 is walking up and down stairs and walking from place to place without any assisted device. K-4 is you running and walking to work, just back to your normal lifestyle. These K-levels are important for you to find meaning for your amputation. It gave me a sense of pride when the physical therapist told me I was a K-4, even though I did not know what it meant. I was just happy to be able to walk on my own again. When something means something to you, you no longer take it for granted, and that is what my amputation truly means to me.

Chapter 5

Finding Your Own Independence

I made this my last chapter because when truly finding your own independence, it allows you to open up the wounds that you only put temporary bandages on. You have to go back and reopen your wounds to allow them to go through the proper healing process. For me, I had not properly dealt with losing my mother to murder at the age of twelve. The news had downplayed how she was murdered as if it was a home on fire. I never understood that for the life of me. It was not until I was lying in the hospital bed fighting for my own life, that I was able to go back to deal with what had haunted me through my childhood all the way to adulthood. Today, I know how to grieve and vent to tell people when I need more time to heal or talk.

Independence does not just mean doing things on your own, but having a purpose for why you are doing the things you are doing. I know this can be a hard pill to swallow, but I believe when you have a purpose for what you're doing that is when it becomes your passion, and it makes you want to continue to make a difference in the lives of others. This is what makes forgiving easy to do because now you do not live with resentment in your heart and now your enemy can become your friend. When you truly let something go, it gives you the independence of freeing your mind, and you no longer live with this burden of how to retaliate with violence but with love. It is easier to give somebody a hug than pick a fight.

Take a moment to think about it… Many of us doubt our Creator so much that we forget the words he said at the beginning of time. He said, "BE and IT IS". Every evening I lay beside my fiancé full of hope and joy that she knows with this amputation that I can still protect my family if a fire breaks out, or if an intruder comes into our home, or even if I need to discipline the kids. We must make every effort to live life with no limitations, so that means making a difference in our community, in our workplace, and in our daily affairs. We should not let anything stop us from being great as we live out our new norm.

One of the things that hold us back is the fear of trusting one another. A lot of us do not trust ourselves because we do not want others to know what we went through. How can we ever be independent if we keep everything hidden inside of us? The more you hurt, the worse it gets because you have not truly dealt with yourself. Finding your independence is letting go of all the assistive devices that stop you from seeing your full potential. James Dixon, a motivational speaker and a good friend of mine, told me when I was walking with a walker, "Man, you will be able to cut your grass again because you can push a damn walker!" Pretty much, he was telling me to let go of the mediocre dreams and goals, and dream of things that I thought would be impossible for me to do as an amputee, such as breaking an Olympic record, having the best walking gait I can have as an amputee, and living my life without no limitations.

Independent living is a great accomplishment after you experience such a tragedy that could have been your final call. So, it is my hope that those of you who are living with fear or doubt about yourselves, you find the courage to bring closure so the true healing process can start. Even if you have an open wound from your childhood, it is better to deal with it than continue to hurt after reading *Five Ways of Healing from an Amputation.*

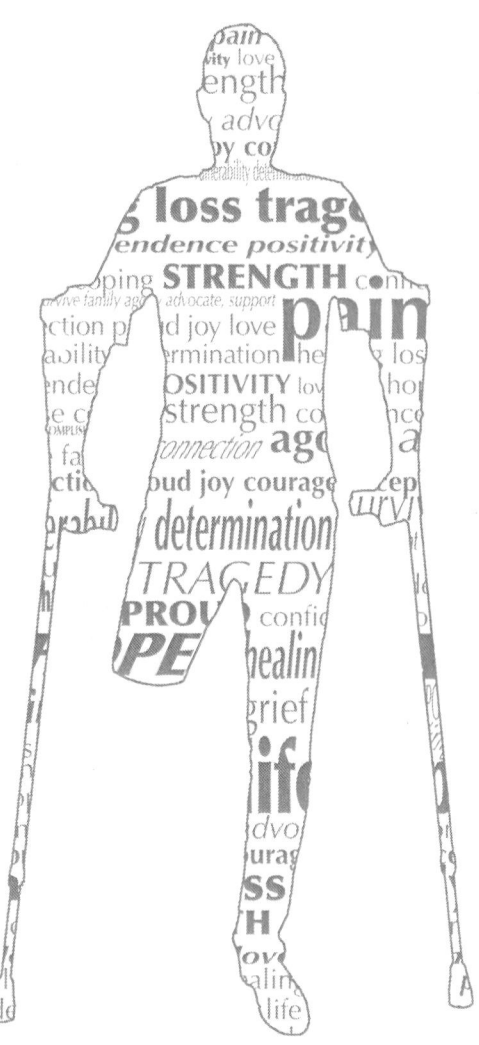

Five Ways of Healing from an Amputation are:

1. Support: Being an Advocate for Yourself
2. Dealing with Depression: Knowing When to Speak Up
3. Learn How to Cope with Phantom Pain
4. Find Meaning for Your Amputation
5. Finding Your Own Independence

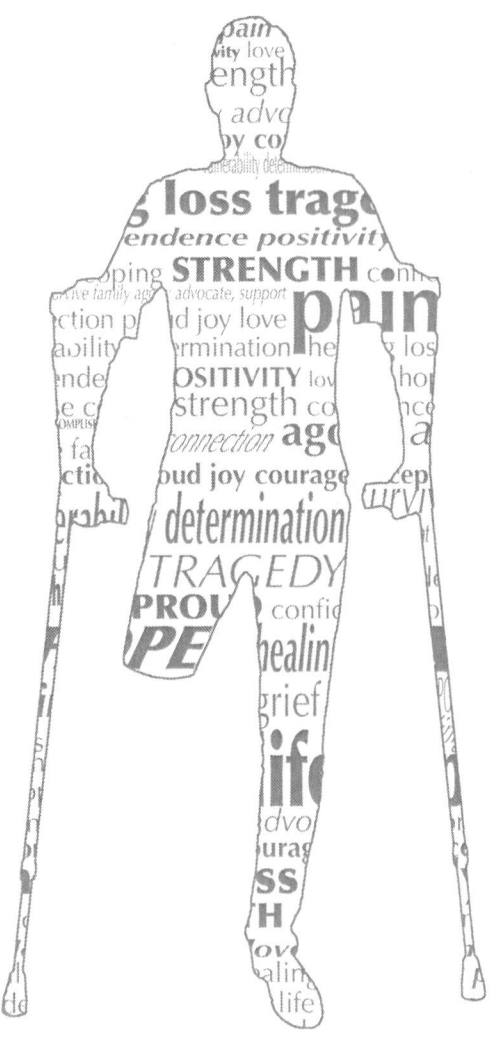

Proud Moments

These moments here almost had me in tears to see how much I had accomplished in three months, but I am truly proud of myself. It is those things that we do that allows us to heal from our amputation.

Anthony's certificate for completing UMSL's Alumni Association 5k Run/Walk

No. 15589

Missouri Credentialing Board

Hereby Certifies that

Anthony Taylor Jr.

has met the qualifications required of a
Certified Peer Specialist
as determined by the Credentialing Board.

Stacy Langendoerfer
_____
Executive Director

Expiration Date **April 30, 2024**

Anthony's certificate as a Certified Peer Specialist

24

				Score
12. Pick up objects off the floor: Pick up a pencil off the floor placed midline 12in in front of foot.	Unable to pick up object and return to standing		= 0	2
	Performs with some help (table, chair, walking aid etc)		= 1	
	Performs independently (without help)		= 2	
13. Sitting down: Ask pt. to fold arms across chest and sit. If unable, use arm or assistive device.	Unsafe (misjudged distance, falls into chair)		= 0	
	Uses arms, assistive device or not a smooth motion		= 1	2
	Safe, smooth motion		= 2	
14. Initiation of gait: (immediately after told to "go")	Any hesitancy or multiple attempts to start		= 0	1
	No hesitancy		= 1	
15. Step length and height: Walk a measured distance of 12ft twice (up and back). Four scores are required or two scores (a. & b.) for each leg. "Marked deviation" is defined as extreme substitute movements to avoid clearing the floor.	**a. Swing Foot**		Prosthesis	Sound
	Does not advance a minimum of 12in	= 0		
	Advances a minimum of 12in	= 1	1	1
	b. Foot Clearance			
	Foot does not completely clear floor without deviation	= 0	1	1
	Foot completely clears floor without marked deviation	= 1		
16. Step Continuity	Stopping or discontinuity between steps (stop & go gait)		= 0	1
	Steps appear continuous		= 1	
17. Turning: 180 degree turn when returning to chair.	Unable to turn, requires intervention to prevent falling		= 0	
	Greater than three steps but completes task without intervention		= 1	1
	No more than three continuous steps with or without assistive aid		= 2	
18. Variable cadence: Walk a distance of 12ft fast as possible safely 4 times. (Speeds may vary from slow to fast and fast to slow varying cadence)	Unable to vary cadence in a controlled manner		= 0	
	Asymmetrical increase in cadence controlled manner		= 1	2
	Symmetrical increase in speed in a controlled manner		= 2	
19. Stepping over an obstacle: Place a movable box of 4in in height in the walking path.	Cannot step over the box		= 0	
	Catches foot, interrupts stride		= 1	2
	Steps over without interrupting stride		= 2	
20. Stairs (must have at least 2 steps): Try to go up and down these stairs without holding on to the railing. Don't hesitate to permit pt. to hold on to rail. Safety First, if examiner feels that any risk in involved omit and score as 0.	**Ascending**			
	Unsteady, cannot do		= 0	
	One step at a time, or must hold on to railing or device		= 1	1
	Step over step, does not hold onto the railing or device		= 2	
	Descending			
	Unsteady, cannot do		= 0	
	One step at a time, or must hold on to railing or device		= 1	1
	Step over step, does not hold onto the railing or device		= 2	
21. Assistive device selection: Add points for the use of an assistive device if used for two or more items. If testing without prosthesis use of appropriate assistive device is mandatory.	Bed bound		= 0	
	Wheelchair / Parallel Bars		= 1	
	Walker		= 2	
	Crutches (axillary or forearm)		= 3	5
	Cane (straight or quad)		= 4	
	None		= 5	

Total Score   AMPnoPRO _____ /43

AMPPRO   43 /47

     21 23 43

Abbreviation: PF = partial foot; TT = transtibial; KD = knee disarticulation; TF = transfemoral; HD = hip disarticulation

Test: ☐ no prosthesis ☐ with prosthesis   Observer: _____ Date: 6/20/22   0745

K LEVEL (converted from AMP score)

AMPnoPRO   ☐ K0 (0-8)   ☐ K1 (9-20)   ☐ K2 (21-28)   ☐ K3 (29-36)   ☐ K4 (37-43)

(15-26)   ☐ K2 (27-36)   ☐ K3 (37-42)   ☒ K4 (43-47)

Anthony completing his K-4 Level

From: **CAF Grants** <cafgrants@challengedathletes.org>
Date: Tue, Jul 19, 2022 at 3:32 PM
Subject: CAF Össur Grant Approved- Prosthetist Contacted
To: CAF Grants <cafgrants@challengedathletes.org>

Hello!

This email is to inform you have been approved for a CAF Össur Grant! We have contacted your prosthetist and provided them with the order form for your Össur Prosthesis(es), granted by CAF. They are now able to place the order for your grant. If you have questions about your grant, please follow up with your prosthetist regarding the status of your order.

Thanks, and again, congratulations on your CAF Össur grant – we are proud to support you!

CAF Grants Team

Jayme Jarvis
Programs Manager
CAF Grants Team

Email of Anthony receiving his CAF grant

From: Anthony <luhtony2903@gmail.com>
Date: September 15, 2022 at 7:02:16 PM CDT
To: Maryann Brickey <mbrickey@slpl.org>
Subject: Re: Loss of Limb Awareness Month (April) Discussion @ Mon Aug 29, 2022

Sound good, thanks for all your help.

Sent from my iPhone

> On Sep 15, 2022, at 4:36 PM, Maryann Brickey <mbrickey@slpl.org> wrote:

Hi Anthony,

We definitely have you on the books for Saturday, April 29th! Currently, we reserved the Auditorium at Central Library as we discussed for a panel discussion, but if you decide to go in a different direction, we still have plenty of time to plan.

Talk to you soon.
Maryann

> On Wed, Sep 14, 2022 at 5:49 PM Anthony <luhtony2903@gmail.com> wrote:
> Ok sound like a plan. We was meeting to just confirm the date for April 29th 2023 and to have a solid place in place.
>
> Sent from my iPhone
>
> > On Sep 14, 2022, at 5:33 PM, Maryann Brickey <mbrickey@slpl.org> wrote:

Emails of Anthony's upcoming event with St. Louis Public Library for
Loss of Limb Awareness Month

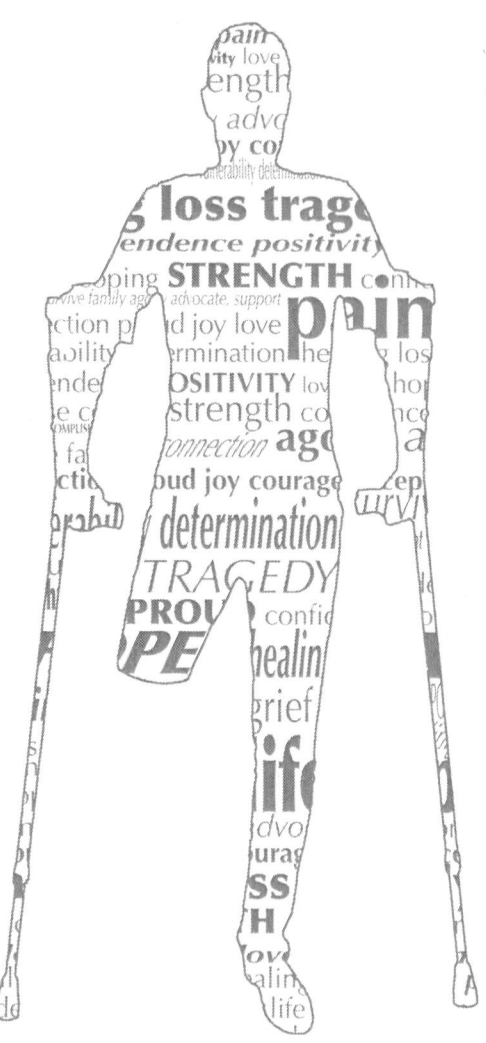

Amp Connections

Amp Connections Support is a nonprofit organization that will contribute to the world by reshaping an amputee's experience after an amputation to ensure that he or she can live a full life after going through the emotional trauma that surgery brings. This book was written to provide amputees, and their families, hope after amputation. For me, I am the only one that is an above-the-knee amputee in my family. I do not want another amputee to experience the harsh reality of coming home from rehab, not knowing who to turn to or what to do. So, I am providing you with reliable resources with real people who care and are happy to help because they helped me. These people are passionate about their work.

Following us on Instagram:
@AmpConnections__

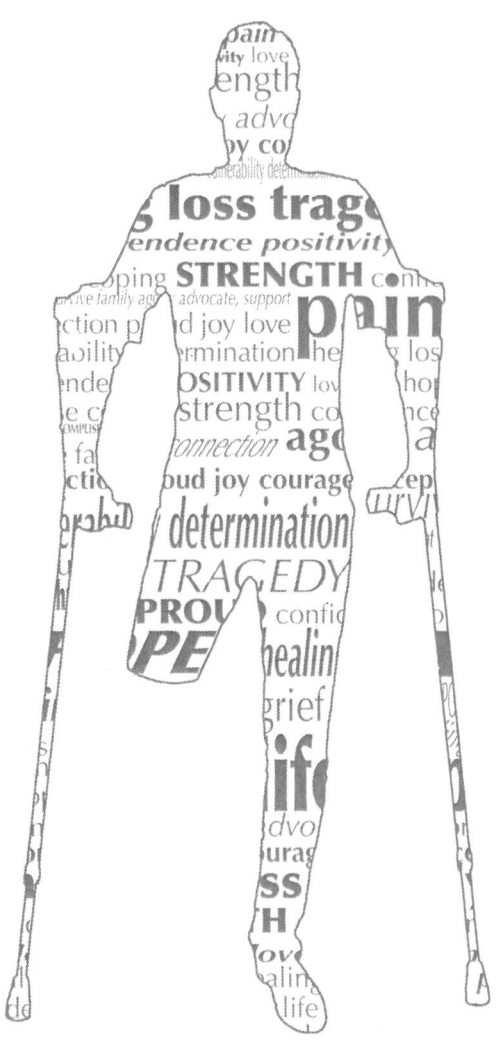

HELPFUL RESOURCES

Challenged Athletes Foundation
9591 Waples St.
San Diego, CA 92121
858-866-0959
https://www.challengedathletes.org/

Consistent Care:
Connecting People to Health
23 North Oaks Plaza, Suite 266
St. Louis, MO 63121
314-932-5644

DASA
1600 Mid Rivers Mall Circle, Suite 2272
St. Peters, MO 63376
636-477-0716
https://dasasports.org/

Premier Prosthetics
AMP'D UP Support Group
343 S. Kirkwood, Suite 200
St. Louis, MO 63122
314-262-8900
https://www.premierpando.com

St. Louis Public Central Library
1301 Olive Street
St. Louis, MO 63103
314- 241-2288

The BRIC
5874 Delmar Blvd
St. Louis, MO 63112
314-624-0398
https://www.thebric.org/

About the Author

Anthony Taylor is a St. Louis native who is passionate about the work he does, and he is always looking for ways to uplift his community and the people around him. Anthony lost his mother at the age of twelve to gun violence, and he is now faced with his own challenges after being shot multiple times and later having his left leg amputated. He has five children that he takes great pride in raising, and he is the thread that holds his family together. After being shot and almost losing his life, he has made the conscious decision to bring about a positive change in society. Anthony received his associate degree from St. Louis Community College and his bachelor's degree in accounting from the University of Missouri- St. Louis. Currently, he is working on obtaining his master's in business. He is using his training to better himself and to help create a program that will restore justice to victims of violence.